SHAL 1

& Ringmore

Chips Barber

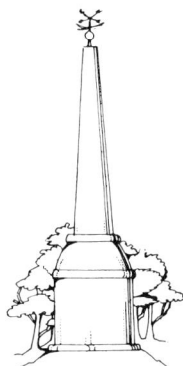

OBELISK PUBLICATIONS

ALSO BY THE AUTHOR:

Ten Family Bike Rides in Devon
Ten Family Walks on Dartmoor • Six Short Pub Walks on Dartmoor
Short Circular Walks in and around Sidmouth • Walks on and around Woodbury Common
Diary of a Dartmoor Walker • Diary of a Devonshire Walker
The Great Little Dartmoor Book • The Great Little Exeter Book
The Great Little Totnes Book • The Great Little Plymouth Book • The Great Little Chagford Book
Made in Devon • The Dartmoor Quiz Book • Place-Names in Devon • An A to Z of Devon Dialect
Dark & Dastardly Dartmoor • The Ghosts of Exeter • Haunted Pubs in Devon
Ghastly & Ghostly Devon • The Lost City of Exeter – Revisited
Exmouth in Colour • Plymouth in Colour • Dawlish and Dawlish Warren in Colour
Beautiful Exeter • Colourful Dartmoor • Colourful Cockington • Topsham in Colour
The South Hams in Colour • Torbay in Colour – Torquay, Paignton, Brixham
Sidmouth Past and Present • Topsham Past and Present • Honiton Past and Present
Seaton & Axmouth • Beer • Branscombe • Colyton & Colyford
Around & About Salcombe • Around & About Teignmouth
Around & About Hope Cove and Thurlestone • Around & About Burgh Island and Bigbury Bay
Around & About Tavistock • Around & About Roborough Down • Around & About Lustleigh
Kingskerswell of Yesteryear (with John Hand)
Dawlish and Dawlish Warren • The South Hams • Torquay • Paignton • Brixham
From The Dart to The Start • Dartmouth and Kingswear
Brixham of Yesteryear, Parts I, II and III • Pinhoe of Yesteryear, Parts I and II
Princetown of Yesteryear, Parts I and II • The Teign Valley of Yesteryear, Parts I and II
Widecombe – A Visitor's Guide • Bickleigh – A Visitor's Guide
Newton Ferrers and Noss Mayo • Along The Otter • Along The Tavy • Along The Avon
Railways on and around Dartmoor • Devon's Railways of Yesteryear
Chagford of Yesteryear • Dartmoor of Yesteryear • Exminster of Yesteryear • Dartmouth of Yesteryear
Heavitree of Yesteryear • Sidmouth of Yesteryear • Whipton of Yesteryear
Plymouth Hoe • Tiverton • The Story of Hallsands • The Story of Dartmoor Prison
The Story of Dawlish Warren • Dawlish of Yesteryear • Discovering Devon…Dawlish
Walk the East Devon Coast – Lyme Regis to Lympstone
Walk the South Devon Coast – Dawlish Warren to Dartmouth
Walk the South Hams Coast – Dartmouth to Salcombe
Walk the South Hams Coast – Salcombe to Plymouth

*We have over 200 Devon titles. For a full list of current titles please send SAE to
Obelisk Publications, 2 Church Hill, Pinhoe, Exeter EX4 9ER. Tel: (01392) 468556.*

PLATE ACKNOWLEDGEMENTS

Thanks to Mavis Piller for pictures on pages 3, 7 (top), 9, 10, 15, 17, 20, 21 (top), 24, 25, 27, 28 (bottom)
and 29; to Nicholas Toyne (Jerome Dessain) for 19 (bottom) and 26 (bottom).
All other illustrations are by or belong to Chips Barber.

ACKNOWLEDGEMENTS

First and foremost, I must thank Robin Mole who knows every nook and cranny of Shaldon, and whose
memories of the place make this a much richer account than could have been envisaged; it is his little
touches that have added spice to the detail. I am extremely grateful to John Pile, who kindly invited me
into his home, took me down the river, and gave me the benefit of his lifetime of experience in Shaldon.
Many thanks also to Richard Ashton, who ran his expert eye over the final proof. His knowledge of the
village's maritime activities is unequalled. Finally, had Jon Rawson not been so darn keen to see a book
about Shaldon and Ringmore, it probably would never have been compiled.

*First published in 2005 by
Obelisk Publications, 2 Church Hill, Pinhoe, Exeter, Devon
Designed and Typeset by Sally Barber
Printed in Great Britain
Avocet Press, Cullompton, Devon*

© Chips Barber/Obelisk Publications 2005

SHALDON
& Ringmore

INTRODUCTION

There may be two Ringmores in Devon (the other is near Bigbury-on-Sea), but there's only one Shaldon. This little book sets out to feature these two Teign estuary-side settlements, largely through memories, old writings and picture postcards, like the view below of

Shaldon's beach in about 1900. Inevitably, Shaldon, with its shops, pubs and many businesses, occupies the lion's share of the book.

My good friend Mavis Piller spent some of her childhood here, about three score and ten years ago, and still has a love affair with the village. She kindly allowed me to dip into her wonderful collection of old picture postcards of the area. Hopefully, in conjunction with some of the more modern scenes that I have taken, they will help to bring the text to life. An attempt has been made to fit the pictures into the appropriate part of the text, but a few are slipped in to make convenient page breaks!

EARLY DAYS – THE CLIFFORDS

Dwarfed by towering hills, the heart of the village lies largely on level land reclaimed from the Teign estuary. It's a splendid location, a fact mirrored by today's relatively high house prices; former fishermen's hovels have now become desirable bijou cottages.

By hook or by crook, by marriage or manipulation, the Carews of Haccombe, from further up the Teign estuary, owned much of the land in this area until 1671. It was then that Lord Clifford made his move and acquired the extensive Parish of St Nicholas, along with other lands.

Therefore, it's no surprise to discover that there are several Clifford connections: the Clifford Arms is a village pub; the local Conservative Club was originally the Clifford Hall; Clifford House, located where Bridge Road meets Torquay Road, was an inn in the 16th century; and on the opposite corner, Lord Clifford's Gothic-styled Hunter's Lodge (circa 1650) is probably the oldest building in the village.

When built, it was located close to the high water mark, but, with reclamation and further development, it now stands well away from the water's edge. Having travelled from Ugbrooke House (the family home), Lord Clifford hunted by day in the marshy lands fringing the Teign and, occasionally, spent his nights at Hunter's Lodge. His servants would light welcoming fires in the stone fireplaces, and the privileged hunting party, having been wined and dined, would contentedly retire to bed. Being an aristocrat was a hard life!

Ultimately, Lord Clifford parted with this property as part of a wedding dowry.

In more recent years the Hunter's Lodge has served several uses: restaurant, private house and antique shop.

WHAT'S IN A NAME?

Various attempts have been made to interpret the meaning of the name 'Shaldon'. One possible geographical deduction is that it was once South Haldon. Knowing the laziness of local speech (or writing) this comes down to Shaldon. Another theory is that 'Shal' is a corruption of 'Shelf' and 'don' means either 'hill' (as it usually does), or 'dune'. Sea-originated beach materials are found just below the surface in lowland Shaldon.

2. Shaldon Bridge, Teignmouth

LOWLAND SHALDON

Until the late 18th century, much of this low-lying area was subject to flooding at times of spring tide. Seemingly, this made it impossible to contemplate any further development. But when money is involved… all things are possible. This former wasteland was intensively developed, The Green being a spacious exception. Consequently, there are several narrow streets and back alleys lined by rows of terraced cottages. However, it should be stressed that Coronation Street in Shaldon is vastly different to that of the famous television series.

Incidentally, there also used to be a Coronation Cottage in the higher part of Horse Lane. It had a thatched roof and an old-fashioned water pump. Although the cottage is gone, the pump was resited at The Green.

Shaldon is such an attractive proposition that developers have constantly threatened to build over every available, or even unavailable, space. Fortunately, in the ranks of the residents there are people equally determined to retain the village's unique character and charm.

The land just to the north of Bridge Road is a case in point; fierce opposition and local pressure ensured that nothing too overwhelming, or out of character, was built. Fortunately, what might have been, hasn't been!

1914 (NOT 1785!)

Several of the pictures in this book date back to the first half of the 20th century. To complement those images, here are a few hard facts, which were published in the County Directory for 1914. Some of the names (but not the personnel!) are still around today: *Shaldon and Ringmore are hamlets forming the parish of St Nicholas, 1 mile south from Teignmouth station on the South Devon section of the Great Western railway... These hamlets, annexed to Teignmouth in 1881, for Union purposes... are picturesquely situated on the south bank of the river Teign, here crossed by a ferry at the Point, and also by a bridge of 34 arches, built chiefly of iron, at a cost of £20,000, under the direction of Mr R. Hopkins, engineer, and opened for traffic June 8, 1827.*

Should we believe all that we read, however factual? It has been suggested that Shaldon Bridge was largely a timber structure, and that it was sheathed in copper to protect it from burrowing worms. Apparently a part of it survives: there is a mooring post not very far from where Shaldon Ferry lands on the estuary beach on this side of the river.

These hamlets are supplied with water from Dartmoor, about 25 miles distant, under the same scheme as the Teignmouth supply, the works at Ringmore, erected by the late Teignmouth Local

Board in 1885, being retained in case of emergency. The church of St Nicholas, near the western extremity of the village was rebuilt in the middle of the thirteenth century and again in 1622 by the Carew family, and at the beginning of the last century the nave was enlarged on the north side by the removal of the north wall and the erection of a rude three-sided structure: the church was until lately a small and unpretending edifice of rough stone... but in 1895 it was restored at the cost of a private benefactor, under the direction of the Rev Gerard H. Ball...

The church of St Peter was commenced in 1893–94 on a site on the main road close to the Shaldon bridge, purchased and given by the vicar (Rev Richard Marsh-Dunn): the work was resumed in 1899, and completed in 1902... The Congregational chapel, erected in 1868, is a building of stone with sittings for 200 persons; the Baptist chapel, built in 1795, has 100 sittings... The Shaldon Lace school was established in 1904 by Miss F. Lancaster Lewis, to help the women and girls and to aid in restoring the lace industry. Lord Clifford of Chudleigh, who is lord of the manor, and Mr J. W. Wood esq are the chief landowners. The soil is limestone, the subsoil is clay. The area of the parish is 578 acres of land and 126 of foreshore...

The directory went on to list hundreds of 'Private Residents' and 'Commercial' listings, enough to show that there were far more shops and tradespeople in Shaldon at that time, although Ringmore didn't have any shops listed, even then! For the dedicated historian, they make interesting reading, but to the ordinary man in the street they simply appear as a rather dull list. However, it is worth selecting a few entries for some names are still locally well known, e.g. William Mole, mason, Dagmar Street; George Orsman junior, butcher, Ringmore Road; George Orsman, butcher; Edward Orsman, market gardener.

CRUISE CONTROL

Although there are not quite as many shops as there were in 1914, there is still a wide range of local businesses, places where local gossip is swiftly passed around. As an outsider, the odd bit of eavesdropping in Harris & Rawson's busy newsagents has proved fruitful to me. Having engaged with some locals in a more meaningful conversation than just the state of the tide or the weather, it led me to a cruise. This was not to the Caribbean, or even around the Med, but upriver to Tesco's in Newton Abbot, and a tad beyond.

The occasion? When pupils are about to graduate from Shaldon School to secondary education, they are treated to a river trip. For more than a decade, this has been organised by local boat owners, and takes place in the pupils' last or penultimate week at junior school. Waiting for no man, the tide dictates the precise timing.

On the chosen day, and having gathered on the beach, the pupils are briefed on how to behave in the boats, and are told what to expect. They are then assigned to various small motor boats, which form a flotilla; the 'Shaldon Armada' then embarks on a cruise under Shaldon Bridge and upstream.

The first port of call is Coombe Cellars, where packed lunches are enjoyed. Afterwards, those with energy to burn are encouraged to play soccer or rounders or both (but not at the same time!)

After this the upstream journey continues. The fleet passes under the towering Kingsteignton By-Pass fly-over, this being supported by thin columns sunk to an amazing depth in the Teign estuary mud and bedrock.

Many flows of water converge above this point and several of the shallow, reed-fringed watercourses are explored. It's the sort of environment where one might expect to see alligators, but fortunately there are none. The various tributaries include the Whitelake Channel, leading to the Stover Canal, and the Teign itself. Those aboard are conveyed past the racecourse as far as the highest navigable point, very much a Devonshire jungle-like environment. Being on the water here is like being in a different world!

One of the regular boatmen, John Pile, kindly allowed me on board for one of these annual adventures. He knows the river well because he does his weekly shopping at Tesco's often by boat, and rightly maintains that it is a much more pleasant and practical experience than travelling by road. Newton Abbot is a traffic hot-spot; there are no traffic jams on the river!

For the maturing pupils, the educational value of the river trip is in an appreciation of the history and heritage that lies in their watery 'backyard'. Tales are related to them of the places passed along the way; it's an experience they are likely to remember for a long time.

SHALDON SCHOOL

The village school at Shaldon has a long history. It opened in 1876, having been built on Home Marsh, land acquired at a cost of £180 from Mr Thomas Brooks, a retired surgeon from Reading.

A school punishment book was rigidly kept between 1911 and 1956; the slightest misdemeanour was usually greeted with a substantial and strategically placed whack of some description. The pupils 'enjoyed' spartan conditions, particularly in winter time when the only form of heating was a smoky stove at the front of the room. Only the girls were allowed to sit near it to derive its immediate warmth.

The most amazing day in the public elementary school's history occurred in 1902 when Mr Alfred Page ('Sniffer'), the ginger-haired headmaster since 1876, was seen walking across Shaldon Bridge, in the direction of his church in Teignmouth. He was never seen again! What happened to him remains a mystery. Perhaps the river has alligators after all!

'Sniffer' was succeeded by the popular Mr Herbert Graham Jackman, a fervent Congregationalist, who held the post until 1939. During the Second World War, the school, whose numbers were boosted by an influx of evacuees, had two female head teachers: Mrs Orchard until 1942 and then Miss Muriel Campling for the following two years. Next in line was Mr David John Williams, whose headship spanned 15 years from 1944. He had the misfortune to suddenly collapse and die. The next incumbent was Robert Maythorne, head from 1959 to 1976, who retired through ill-health. Mr Vear took on the mantle.

LOCAL NICKNAMES

In the first half of the 20th century it was a common practice to bestow imaginative nicknames on one's contemporaries: Tabso, Gravy-Eye, Buck, Putty-Dotty, Blinker, Sniffy, Chubby-Toes, Shrimpy, Star-gazer, Calico Jack and Dummy being just some from Shaldon.

'Dummy' Bennett lived in Poorhouse Lane (now School Lane) in the early part of the 20th century. As its former name suggests, this is where the ne'er do wells were obliged to live, in three Dickensian-styled poor houses. The administration of these somewhat insanitary properties was under the auspices of the Board of Guardians, not all of them angels in disguise. The County Council took over the function in 1929.

This scene is of Moles Cottage, which was demolished in the mid-1920s, the sort of property that, with a lot of tender loving care (and d-i-y) would be worth a small fortune today. Standing at the door is Mrs Mole. The Tothill boys, George and Jack, are standing on the left-hand side of the picture postcard view, which was published by Currie and Cliffe Ltd of Teignmouth. This firm was responsible for some excellent and unusual views of the district; as collectors' items, these now command many hundreds of times their original face value.

The Beach, Shaldon Teignmouth

George Young & Sons Ltd of Teignmouth were also in the picture postcard publishing business and, conveniently, the two Tothill lads were around again to pose. Although the picture was probably taken about 1907, this card to London wasn't posted until 1913.

Shaldon, Fore Street

NOT AMUSED!

Shaldon has always had a reputation as being a 'laid-back' place. A case in point occurred when it came to marking the Diamond Jubilee of Queen Victoria (1897). A modest drinking fountain was planned, to be sited close to Hunter's Lodge. Having collected subscriptions to erect such a structure, the villagers waited patiently for this new source of liquid refreshment. However, it was so long in the making that it became the butt of local jokes, one of them practical.

Apart from being a greengrocer, Mr William Tothill, of 5 The Green, was also the village crier in those days; his stentorian tones could be heard on numerous occasions. A small number of locals thought that they would have a laugh at his expense. They informed him that the fountain was nearing completion and asked him if he would 'do the honour' of unveiling it. For that essential air of mystery that pertains to occasions like this, a large tarpaulin was drawn over the fountain site. Having made the official

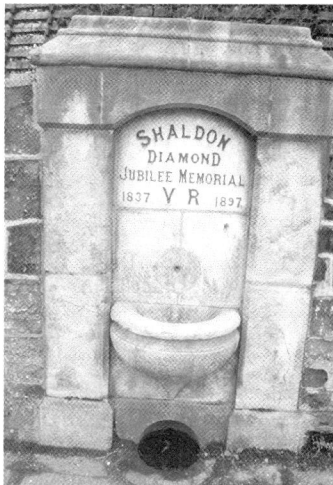

pronouncement, the unsuspecting Mr Tothill then removed the covering. History does not record what his words or reaction were, but there was no pristine drinking fountain, merely a rusty mug chained to the wall!

As can be seen from the photograph, the villagers did get their Jubilee Fountain, but not for some while. This recent photograph shows it has long since ceased serving its intended function.

DAGMAR STREET

Wych or Wyche Cottage, situated in Dagmar Street, is shown here garlanded in flowers. The narrow road in which it stands is named after a Scandinavian builder who took a shine to Shaldon and spent much time here, quite probably enjoying the mild winters.

But not everything you see in this street is what it appears to be… One cottage looks very old, but has a wall of polystyrene blocks concealed beneath rendering, after the original cob wall collapsed.

RINGMORE'S CHURCH OF ST NICHOLAS

On the banks of the Teign, the small church of St Nicholas is located in Ringmore. This is what was written in the *Church Monthly* in April 1892: *Our* not *pretty little church was as usual very prettily decorated on Easter Day by the following ladies: Mrs Marsh-Dunn and Miss Boden, the*

altar; Miss Lambert, the font; Mrs Fiddian, the pulpit; the Misses Ball, the choir stalls; the Misses Lucas and Graeme, the north window; the Misses Martin, the east-aisle window; the Misses Sinabaldi, Nethersole, and Woodford, the west-aisle window and gallery pillars. Many thanks are due to these kind workers, as also to those who gave flowers, etc.

But the church had a pressing need. This appeared in the same edition. *WANTED. A small harmonium for use in our Sunday School and for Choir practices. In fact, it is absolutely necessary. Our present one has done its duty and is quite worn out; it has been called a "wheeze-box," but now it refuses even to wheeze unless compelled by main force, and our Organist says that after a practice last week he felt as if he had taken a five-mile walk.*

Will any one or more of our kind ladies come forward to beg subscriptions for this most desirable and necessary object? I feel sure they will.

Despite the lack of decent musical hardware, the church had a star student. *Among other successes of different pupils under the tuition of our Organist, Mr F. T. Beer, we are glad to be able to congratulate him upon a pupil of his, Miss Sallie Harvey, having successfully passed the preliminary examination of the London College of Music.*

This appeared in the press on 21 October 1895: *The quaint little parish church, which for many years has been a source of considerable attraction and interest, from an archaeological point of view, to visitors to Teignmouth and the neighbourhood, will soon, as regards its original shape and form, be a thing of the past. The sacred edifice originally consisted of a nave and south aisle. It was built in the middle of the 13th century, long before the existence of the present Shaldon, for the accommodation of about 60 fishermen and their families, and was restored in 1622. About 70 years ago this interesting little church was completely destroyed by the pulling down of the north wall, and the erection of a hideous structure in its place. Since the opening of the new church in the Bridge Road in July, 1894, the old church at Ringmore has only been used as a mortuary*

chapel in connection with the churchyard in which it stands, and for an early celebration of Holy Communion on the 4th Sunday of every month. Some months ago the Rev R. M. Marsh-Dunn, vicar of the parish, received an offer from an anonymous donor to restore the church to its original condition. A parish meeting was called, and it was unanimously agreed to accept the kind offer, and to commence the work as soon as possible. The alterations to be made consisted of pulling down the modern additions, and throwing the ground on which they stand into the churchyard, inserting three new windows to match the present St Nicholas one, and adding a west door. The chapel is 42 ft long and 17 ft wide, and the floor is covered with Belgium diagonal black and white tiles. There are eight coloured windows, including a large beautifully stained one, over the altar representing the crucifixion, and two smaller ones near the east end containing the figures of St Nicholas and St Agnes. The chapel will accommodate about 60 persons. The work will be completed about Christmas, and, when finished, will be one of the prettiest mortuary chapels in the diocese.

LIQUFRUTA

Lying peacefully at rest at Ringmore is a man who links the two communities of Ringmore and Shaldon. William Newcombe Homeyard was the inventor of the cough syrup known as Liqufruta. It made him a rich man; enjoying the 'fruits' of his labour, he lived with his wife at Ness Cottage.

He passed away on 6 July 1927 and, unknowingly, caused a stir. Clearly proud of her husband's achievements, his widow wished to acknowledge the cough mixture on his headstone (a cross). The local vicar wouldn't entertain such a notion. It was not a place for an advertisement! But Maria Laetitia Kempe Homeyard was an astute woman. She knew the limitations of her priest; she overcame the problem by resubmitting a 'Latin' word in its stead. The ignorant cleric did not have the wit to recognise that "Aturfuqil" was Liqufruta spelled backwards!

TEIGNMOUTH FROM BOTANICAL GARDENS, SHALDON   G 9286

HOMEYARD'S BOTANICAL GARDENS

Homeyard's name also lives on high above Shaldon. Homeyard's Botanical Gardens lie on the estuary side of the main coast road as it rises above the village on its way out of town towards

Torquay. In 1928 Mrs Homeyard bought the land for the informal, originally private, terraced gardens. Thomas Rider was employed as architect to design them, but the task of laying out and landscaping was entrusted to William Sears. He did a magnificent job, installing the pond and planting rockeries with yucca, berberis, escallonia, phlomis and so on. From here there is a splendid view towards Teignmouth.

The garden includes this summer house built in the form of a castle. Descended from the famous Cornish family of Kempe, Maria entertained friends with tea-parties and games of bridge here. She died in 1944. In 1950 Teignmouth Town Council purchased the gardens; five years later they were officially opened to the public.

SHALDON'S CHURCH OF ST PETER

Until the early 1890s Anglican residents of Shaldon had to traipse all the way to St Nicholas for Sunday worship, a situation that was far from ideal, particularly in inclement weather. The solution was found in the 1890s:

A church has long been needed by the parishioners of Shaldon, which has grown in the last 50 years. The old church, which is of 13th century date, is a very interesting specimen of Devonian architecture, and as it was too small for the growing population it was unfortunately enlarged in the 18th century, very much to the detriment of the old fabric. But as this church is situated about a mile from the mass of the inhabitants, it has been found necessary to erect a new church in the midst of the parish. The architect for the building is Mr Edmond Sedding, of Plymouth.

On Friday week the Bishop of Exeter laid the foundation stone of a new church... The growth of Shaldon has been considerable, having now a population of close on 1300. During the past three months the work of excavation and laying the footings for the walls has been going on. The committee have decided to proceed with the work as far as funds will permit, and, so far, they intend building the aisle walls complete, and roofing over the entire area with temporary iron.

Even with this part of the undertaking, extra expense has been necessitated on account of the sandy nature of the soil on which the building stands. The aisle walls are to be built of a dark red sandstone, the other dressings are to be of limestone... The cost of the first portion of the building is estimated at £1,300 of which about £800 has been subscribed. The balance (£500) has been advanced on loan by the vicar, the interest having been generously promised by a non parishioner. The choir and clergy robed in the public rooms and marched in procession to the site, singing, "Blessed City, Heavenly Salem." the Rev R. M. Marsh-Dunn, Vicar, officiated. Shaldon Choir was assisted by members of at St Michael's choir, Teignmouth. ... The Bishop laid the stone on which it was inscribed: 'Laus Deo - this stone was laid by the Lord Bishop of Exeter, July 21st, 1893.'

St Peter's was completed two years later and the opening ceremony was not without incident: *At the opening of a new church at Shaldon on Thursday, by the Bishop of Exeter, his lordship having performed the dedication ceremony retired to the vestry at the commencement of the Communion Service, and remained there until the conclusion of the Creed. Then he entered the pulpit, looking extremely pale. In a somewhat tremulous voice he gave out as his text the last verse of Psalm xc, "The prayer of Moses." He had been speaking three or four minutes, and was emphasising the power of beauty, particularly in character, when he suddenly stopped, and then said, "If you will bear with me for my weakness a few moments, and sing another of the hymns on the form, I will return." Thereupon he returned hastily to the vestry, where he was quickly followed by Dr Bell, of Shaldon, and others. They found his lordship somewhat seriously indisposed, and attacked by a fainting fit. The Rev R. M. Marsh-Dunn immediately gave out the*

hymn, *"We love the place, O God,"* and at its conclusion the Bishop re-entered the pulpit, and after regretting that he had had to interrupt their meditations, proceeded to say that he thanked God for the substantial walls within which they were met, and for the generous gifts received. The Bishop then returned to the vestry again, and the service proceeded. His lordship subsequently drove to the station, being unable to remain for the luncheon.

The church is a monument to the enterprise of the vicar, the Rev R. M. Marsh-Dunn. The old church at Ringmore, interesting from an archaeological point of view, has long been unsuited for public service, but the present vicar was the first to take definite steps for the erection of a church nearer the great bulk of the 1300 residents at Shaldon, and where the parishioners could worship *in comfort. Despite opposition and difficulties, Mr Marsh-Dunn has carried through his scheme to an almost successful issue. He and his family have been the largest contributors. About two years ago Gowrie House, splendidly situated on the banks of the Teign at the Shaldon end of the bridge, came into the market, and the vicar purchased it, had the building demolished, and gave the site for the erection of the Church. Plans were prepared by Mr E. Sedding... and as soon as £1,000 of the necessary £3,000 had been subscribed the work was taken in hand. The Church would have been opened earlier, but the work was impeded in the spring by the demolition of the temporary roof by a severe gale.*

In those early years, the choir were required to wear slippers to soften the sound when they walked across the marble floor. There was even a small orchestra to play for full-house congregations every Sunday.

The Rev Richard Marsh Marsh-Dunn was a very forceful man whose word was gospel and who imposed his strength of character on the village, usually for the good of all. He was a typical Victorian who stood no nonsense and was a strong disciplinarian. One can imagine his horror when Kensit preachers of the Protestant Truth Society arrived on his patch. Their 'guru' – John Kensit – died in 1902 from his injuries two weeks after a religious riot at Birkenhead. The same level of violent reaction was not matched here, but irate choir members were quick to throw the Kensit preachers headlong into the River Teign! Following their duckings, they soon departed the scene.

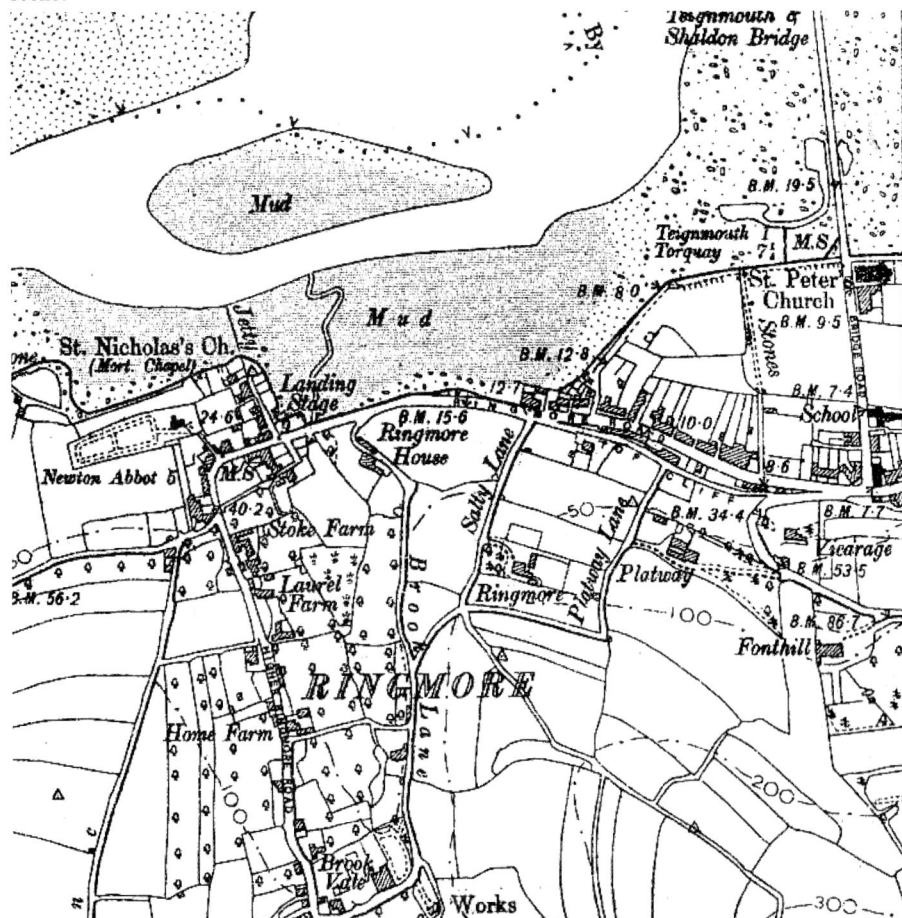

FISHING FOR FUN

An early 20th-century publication called *Devonia* included this under the general heading of "Health and Pleasure Resorts of Devon": *Shaldon, to those who may not know of its whereabouts, lies on the far side of the river Teign from Teignmouth, and is cosily situated. My object in writing this is to give an account of our varied fishings, as I do not know of any place where such a variety can be obtained within so short a distance. After a lapse of some years we decided to visit Shaldon again, and took a small house on the front. It was quite cheerful to see some of the old faces, and to know that former visits had not been forgotten.*

One of the first familiar faces to meet us was that of genial Captain Matthews, the senior Trinity pilot, who immediately asked the writer to go fishing for mackerel at sunrise next morning. The invitation was accepted. Being called early, having had some tea and bread and butter, out we went. We reached to and fro the bay, getting back in time for breakfast, bringing forty-seven mackerel with us.

The next thing to do was to engage a boat and man for our ordinary amusement, and we settled with the owner of the "Hiordis," who showed us capital sport. He was a really good trier for finding, and keen on getting us sport. The "Hiordis" is a 16-ft. dinghy, with centre keel and carrying jib, main, and mizzen sails, and is a very handy little boat. We sailed out in it for mackerel early mornings and late afternoons, having some fine catches, the largest, in a four hours' run, being one hundred and ninety-seven to two lines.

The boatman told us what to try from day to day. When the spring tides were on and the sprat sands on the Teignmouth side uncovered we would go across with rakes and dig for sand eels. This was very great fun, especially for the ladies. As soon as the sand is turned over and a sand

Ringmore from Shaldon Bridge, Teignmouth

eel is seen it has to be grabbed at once, for if it gets its sharp nose in the wet sand it is gone like a streak of lightning. The large sand eels are very good eating, and the small ones are kept alive for bait. We used the small ones mostly for trailing for bass in the mouth of the river, at slack low tides. The chief coastguard there was a man called Murray, one of the best bass fishermen to be found. He would go out and paddle about and almost make sure of a catch when other boats could do nothing.

The small sand eels were used again for a "Bull-Tow," which is a long line of about 100 feet, and at every 18 inches is tied a short line of eight inches with a hook attached. These hooks are baited with sand eel, and the line is weighted. It is then put across the tideway, the ends being drawn out to the fullest capacity. A float is attached to one end, so as to spot it when wanted. This is let down for an hour or two and then hauled up, when eels, occasionally a small conger, flounders, and bass are often landed.

The Salty

Hotel
New Quay
B.M. 11·5

Hotel
·13·9
South View
THE DEN

B.M. 13·0   B.M. 19·8

TEIGNMOUTH
PIER
Pavilion   Landing Stage

Coastguard Station
Breakwater
Boatbuilding Yard

Powderham Terrace
B.M. 15·2

Meteorological Station

RIVER TEIGN

B.M. 14·5
Lighthouse
Breakwater
Lifeboat House

B.M. 20·1

3·8   Boatbuilding Yard
Fort View
B.M. 12·2

B.M. 9·2
A Quay

Ferry

The Point

H.W.M.O.T.

L.W.M.O.T.

L.W.M.O.T.

Coal Stages
B.M. 12·0

Spratt Sand

North View — 50
SHALDON
Common Lane

Shaldon House
B.M. 11·3

Breakwater

Torquay Road — 100

Pole Sand

Horse Lane
Ness Cottage
B.M. 135·3

200   B.M. 174·6

Lodge

The Ness

F.B.

Packet Head Hill
300

Lodge

Dunmore
Subway

400 Yards
300
B.M. 227·0

O   L   A   S

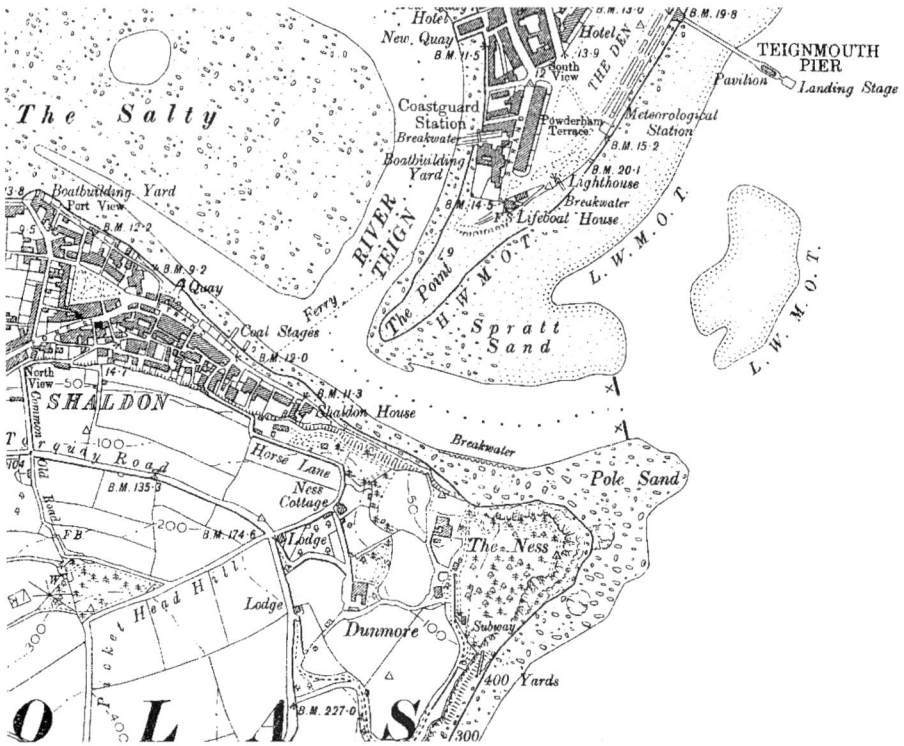

Sometimes we would hire a small seine and at low tides shoot off the pier, bar and Ness Beach, and round one or two of the coves towards Babbacombe, and in one day have landed, in addition to bass, mackerel, dabs, etc., as many as twenty-seven mullet. This is good exercise for all who take part in it, and very enjoyable.

In the evenings we would go out after dinner and anchor in the tideway, and fish for conger, using pilchards or half a mackerel for bait, and have caught five congers in one evening. We took a lady out one evening for this sport. She caught the first one, and when she, with our help, got it in the boat, she nearly went over the other side to get out of the way.

Another good form of sport was to go out prawning at night time with drop nets. These are nets of fine mesh, tied to a thin iron hoop, and baited by tying gurnet or some similar fish to the cross strings, and attaching a line with a float to the centre. We used to have about twenty-four of these nets. They were dropped around the rocks and left for some time, and were then hauled up in rotation, and dropped back as soon as any prawns were shaken out into the well of the boat. We did not use the "Hiordis," but had a special boat for these occasions. It was our luck to catch one or two lobsters occasionally in these nets. We have on going out sometimes put a trammel across the tideway, and picked this up on way back. The boatman would have a copper boiling by the time we got back, and the prawns were dropped in at once, and brought to us nice and fresh in the early morning, ready to send away to friends or to eat ourselves.

At low spring tides a favourite amusement was to picnic on the beach around the Ness, when the menkind would wade around the rocks towards Babbacombe with hand nets for prawns, and these days were always enjoyable.

If the weather were rough, and we could not get outside we have gone up the river fishing for eels or flounders, or around the piles of the harbour pier for prawns, and it's surprising what a lot of these latter can be got by scraping up the piles or the hulls moored in the harbour.

Another day we would go out dabbing, using mussels for bait. For this we anchored and the roll of the boat seemed to upset some of our guests more than the sailing.

Friends of ours, who were staying at Exeter from Halifax, would not believe all we told them about our varied fishing excursions, so we arranged for them to spend a day with us. They came down to Teignmouth by an early morning train. We were waiting for them and started them on their day's pleasure by putting them to dig for sand eels. It was great fun to see the way they went at it, after the first start, the ladies being as keen as the men. We had an early lunch and took the menkind out mackereling and brought them back with a catch of seventy.

After dinner we took them out for a short while prawning with the sink or drop nets, and our catch was two-hundred and forty-six and one lobster. We sent them back to Exeter thoroughly converted and full of their day's pleasure. Visitors are always keen on watching the big seine shooting for salmon at low water, and excitement used to run high, both with the visitors and fishermen when the seine was nearly in shore, and the fish could be seen trying to get out of the nets. Perhaps eight or ten seines would be shot, one after the other, and covering the whole of the Shaldon shore and Salty on each side of the bridge.

SALMON FISHING AT SHALDON

The fishing was varied by boat trips to Coombe Cellars, to which place cockle and cream teas are peculiar; drives across the high road to Babbacombe and Torquay, steamer trips from Teignmouth to other seaside places along the coast, Exmouth, Seaton, Sidmouth, Torquay, Dartmouth and drives over Dartmoor… all help to make an enjoyable holiday.

The bathing around "Ness Beach" is very satisfactory and at low tide one can walk out a long way. At high tide one is soon in deep water. Mixed bathing is indulged in, tents being used as there are no machines…

For a quiet and enjoyable holiday, to anyone who is fond of sea fishing, I can thoroughly recommend Teignmouth or Shaldon as a centre.

This lengthy article dealt entirely with local waters. It should be remembered that many Shaldon fishermen, like those of Teignmouth, travelled thousands of miles to the cod fishing grounds, the Grand Banks of Newfoundland, in on order to make a living. It was the mainstay of the local economy. Captain Potter, of Potter's Mooring (see page 28), was one such entrepreneur. Working on the concept of economic journeys, he would load up with local clay, sail to Liverpool and unload. Reloaded with salt, from Cheshire, he would then sail to Newfoundland for the cod fishing. Having caught a boatload, he would sail back to the Mediterranean, where there was a ready market for his wares. His round journey would be completed when his fruit-laden vessel returned to the shores of Devon. Then the cycle of trade would begin again.

THE VILLAGE GREEN

And talking of centres, the village green was a very different place in the past, when it was the

practice for fishermen to dry their nets here. Many years ago, when it was mooted that a bowling green was going to be created on part of it, there was panic by those living on its perimeter. They were worried about the possibility of their windows being broken. It would take a wildly erratic and errant bowler to manage this feat in such a terrestrial sport!

In return for losing this valuable space, the villagers gained an amenity that has served them well for years. Sheltered by attractive surrounding properties, this must surely be one of the best places to play this sociable game.

Some locals maintain that house owners had, and still have, the right to park their horse-drawn conveyances around The Green. It's another matter to convince the local traffic warden!

RUSTIC ROUNDABOUTS?

It was the custom once for farmers to escort their cows from outlying farms through the streets of Shaldon and down to the Strand Dairy (16 The Strand) to be milked. The downside of having fresh milk almost on the doorstep was that these creatures were not house-trained. Some Shaldon folk still remember the streets being liberally splattered with animal droppings. Children who rolled their hoops along the road had to treat the enormous cowpats, some almost as big as dustbin-lids, like mini-roundabouts. On at least one occasion, Bellamy's coal lorry skidded on this slippery 'hot-top' and ended up facing back the way that it came! Around that time, buildings housing pigs and cows were found in what we would regard today as the most unlikely of places, tucked away in the back streets of the village. For example, Edward Wakeham had a number of 'agricultural' buildings in Dagmar Street, on the site where the Over-60s Club is now located. For the community, it meant that with a relatively high number of local butchers, who kept their animals in such outbuildings, the meat was fresh at the point of sale. The slaughterhouse was sited not very far away, close to the site of the present Londis supermarket.

SHALDON FERRY

It's impossible to understate the importance of the Shaldon Ferry. An ancient service, it merits due consideration. This appeared in the press on 14 November 1949: *For the first time since the ferry service was introduced 123 years ago Teignmouth and Shaldon ferry has changed ownership with its purchase by Mr W. J. L. Powell, of Okehampton at an undisclosed figure.*

The ferry rights were acquired in 1826 by Shaldon Bridge Company, which had been endeavouring to dispose of the ferry since Shaldon Bridge was taken over by Devon County Council and freed from tolls.

Before the ferry could be sold to Mr Powell, the Bridge Company had to promote a special Parliamentary Bill which was passed earlier this year.

The concessions granted in 1826 carried an obligation that the rights should be sold only to a local authority, but Teignmouth Urban Council would make no offer. The new Bill enabled the sale to an individual.

Until the advent of motor boats the ferry was operated with rowing-boats painted in black and white squares, the decorations still in use.

In difficult weather and tides, the crossing sometimes took thirty minutes compared with three minutes today. Boatmen were allowed to take 12 passengers and worked from 6 am to 9 pm in the summer for £1 per week.

Mr A. J. Hocking who has known the ferry since a boy and has been manager for the last ten years, cannot recollect any serious accident in its history. He adds that the usefulness was shown in the fact that 100,000 passengers were carried in August.

The only increase in fares since the ferry started has been from a 1d to one and ha'pennies. The Bill enables further increases of another penny.

The ferry has been formally handed over to Mr Powell, who served in the Royal Navy for many years.

Probably dating back to the 13th century, and much older than suggested above, the ferry service has witnessed changes. It was motorised in 1909. Prior to this it had a mast and sail and the ferryman had bulging Popeye-style muscles. As the new ferry boasted port and starboard lights, one of the local wags exclaimed that "We're getting more like London every day!"

In April 1951 this appeared in a local paper: *A Ministry of Local Government and Planning inquiry at Teignmouth was told yesterday that over 100,000 passengers are carried in ferries between Shaldon and Teignmouth in August, and in July and September the number was between 70,000 and 80,000.*

Mr W. J. L. Powell, of 12, The Green, Shaldon, was appealing against the refusal of the Council to permit the erection of a boat-house with dwelling accommodation over, at River-view, Shaldon. The inspector was Mr J. B. Fairchild.

Mr R. E. Millman, of Exeter, for Mr Powell, said he owned a plot of land which had been used from time immemorial as a base for the storing and repairing of ferries. The present structure was very dilapidated and the runway would need repair in the near future. In addition there would be an increase in the size and power of the ferry boats and this meant that some major alteration would have to be made to enable them to be serviced and for stores and equipment.

There was no alternative site in Shaldon from which the ferry could be operated. The service was part of the life of the village and enabled people to bring their money into the Ness Estate and help trade generally.

The reason for the Council's refusal was that the proposal would prejudice the future planning of the area, River-view to the river, which should remain free from building development.

For the planning authority, Mr J. E. Knapman, Clerk of the County Planning Committee, said it opposed the erection of a two-storey building on top of the workshop. Mr Powell was living within a stone's throw of his business and although the ferry had been there for nearly 130 years no previous owner had found that he needed a dwelling-house on top of the workshop…

There have been many ferrymen throughout the years: George Onion, Joe Onion (the locals knew their Onions!), Fred Westlake, Bill Westlake, Norman Williams, Sammy Sampson, George Tothill, Sid Wolfe, Fred Drewe, Henry Hitchcock, Fred Delbridge, 'Plum' Morritt and Charlie Soaper. The latter was ferryman for 33 years, so he knew the way across pretty well by the end!

In the late 1980s, Brian Baldock, the local traffic warden, travelled to the resort on the Shaldon Ferry. For a while this ploy provided an element of surprise. Unsuspecting illegally parked vehicles suddenly found 'fixed penalty' notes attached to their windscreens. To combat the obvious sting of the 'yellow peril', surveillance measures were taken to observe the one-man invasion. Various forms of audio and visual links were established to provide an early warning system. News travels fast in Shaldon; bad news, even faster!

LOCAL PIRATES?

At one time the ferry had unofficial competition – a pirate vessel run by the Sharland brothers. They tried to outwit officialdom by employing the technicality of not accepting tolls by hand. They trusted passengers to leave the due remittance on the seat when disembarking. Nevertheless, they were successfully sued by the ferry company, who were awarded the minimum damages of a farthing (there were 960 in a pound).

Pre-decimilisation pennies were a lot bigger and heavier than the coins in use today, a point to consider in this tale: when the Sharlands went to collect a newly built boat from Teignmouth, they paid for it in cash – all pennies! Boats were costed out at a pound per foot, so it must have been a very weighty payment that was handed over!

Charlie Sharland ('Chubby-Toes') and his bachelor brothers, Emmanuel and Henry, lived with Maud, one of their two spinster sisters, in Middle Street. The brothers could be identified by their hats: Emmanuel and George, another brother, favoured a peaked cap, the others sported bowlers. Emmanuel was the last of the family to go, a rather straight-laced man who became something of a fixture on the estuary beach; he was easily recognised in his old-fashioned frock coat and the boots which he never took off. It is said that when he passed away, they had to cut them off his feet!

CROWNING GLORY?

Although Shaldon can no longer be regarded as a true port, there have been various comings and goings of inter-coastal craft. In the first decade of the last century, three colliers would regularly discharge their cargoes at three wooden jetties. A few local 'lumpers' were employed to shovel the coal into wheel-barrows to take it to nearby stores. One of these was located almost opposite the Ferry Boat Inn, which, in those days, was called The Crown. Crown Square is nearby.

The pub was not quite the refined place that it is now. Spittoons were placed at regular spots around the bar to enable the old men who chewed tobacco to test their accuracy when issuing oral projectiles!

TAXI!

With its narrow, twisting streets, and occasional awkwardly parked vehicles, the village is not the easiest place to drive around, although some folks have had no choice. This photograph from 1933 shows the former Bridge Road Garage (tel no. 55) with its state-of-the-art Shellmex petrol pumps. Proudly standing in front of his premises is Mr W. Ravenhill, who ran a taxi service from here.

THE NESS

The Ness overlooks waterfront Shaldon from on high. From its summit there are also views eastwards along the South Devon coast to Teignmouth, Dawlish, Dawlish Warren and beyond. Apparently, the trees on the Ness were planted in honour of Queen Victoria attaining her silver jubilee year (1862), although a few sources suggest other dates.

Lying snugly beneath this great red cliff, Ness House was built in 1810 as a summer residence for Lord Clifford, whose family owned it until 1895. For a while it was rented by the famous, much-travelled metallurgist Henry Forbes Julian, who also maintained a London residence. He was a founder member of the Royal Automobile Club. A globe-trotter, he was an active member of both the Torquay Natural History Society and

THE NESS CAFE, SHALDON

the Devonshire Association, these having been founded by his future father-in-law, William Pengelly FRS FGS, the eminent geologist of Torquay. Hester, William's daughter, was also a member, and it was always on the cards that they would marry. Unfortunately, he was one of the ill-fated 1,513 people who lost their lives when the *Titanic* sank off the Grand Banks of Newfoundland. There is a memorial to him at Upton Church, Torquay, which reads: *Ad Majorem Dei Gloriam. This tablet is erected by a wide circle of friends in affectionate memory of HENRY FORBES JULIAN Member of the Institution of Mining and Metallurgy; Born Ascension Day, 9th May 1861, Married in this church, 30th October, 1902, Passed away 15th April, 1912. During the whole of his working life he laboured at the solution of metallurgical problems in three continents, and both by his writings and practical skill, exercised an influence which will long endure. He was amongst those who gave their lives for others in the disaster which befell the RMS TITANIC. This heroism and self-denial called forth admiration from the Throne to the cottage. "Greater love hath no man than this, that a man may lay down his life for his friends."*

Hester had been ill at the time of the sailing, and her husband had advised her to stay at home. He was originally scheduled to leave a week earlier on another ship, but was obliged to put back the date by the effects of a national coal strike. His body was never found.

Hester lived in Torquay until her death in 1934. She was then buried alongside her parents William and Lydia Pengelly at Hele Road cemetery.

Past owners of the unusual Ness Hotel include the grand-sounding Captain Fitzmaurice Crichton, Colonel Brine, and Mr Holder, a member of a notable shipping family.

Nell Gwyn (c.1650–1687), mistress of Charles II, is reputed to have stayed at the nearby Ness Farmhouse. She went from selling oranges outside the Drury Lane Theatre to being a comedy actress on its stage. We all have to start somewhere!

Based in a woodland setting at The Ness, the Shaldon Wildlife Trust is open throughout the year. Billing itself as the "Best Little Zoo in the West", it has many rare and endangered species, and is a breeding centre for them. A registered charity, it cares for over 30 species of animals, specializing in small mammals. It makes a most interesting visit for families, particularly those with young children.

The road from the Ness to Shaldon was private until 1949; it was originally gated at Shaldon House on Marine Parade. If you look closely at the old postcard opposite, you will just be able to see this gateway lying to the left of the property in the centre distance.

SHALDON REGATTA

The annual Regatta has been staged almost continuously since 1817. Races originally involved working boats – luggers, fishing craft, sailing boats, punts, gigs and rowing boats of various lengths. Twelve to 13-foot rowing boats abounded in Shaldon because of local conditions. Washed by a stiff current, the steeply profiled sandy beach provided boatmen with a daunting challenge every time boats had to be removed from the water. Therefore small boats were preferred.

In the early years of regattas, it was necessary to introduce handicapping; this caused some heated arguments. It was inevitable that, sooner rather than later, after such intense rivalry, a standard design and size would prevail.

The evolution went something like this. There was a consensus that Morgan Giles built the fastest punts: both John Pile and Chris Clarance won the men's single sculls in *Little Nell* at the age of 17 – one in 1948, the other in 1964 – and similar Giles' boats always acquitted themselves well. By 1964 competing boats had to be 12ft or under, with a 4ft beam. The smaller punts thus evolved into the regular racing rowing boat. Today it is enshrined in the 11ft regatta boat.

Trewman's Exeter Flying Post reported this on 22 June 1848: *Shaldon Regatta took place on the 15th inst, when flags of all colours were hoisted the whole length of the Strand facing the water, and also on the vessels and boats in the harbour, having a pretty appearance. The Shaldon Temperance Band was in attendance...*

But there have been some sad times as well. A tragedy occurred in September 1864: *Shaldon had its regatta on Monday last, but a sad accident marred the pleasures of the day. The Signal gun was placed on the land end of the jetty, and the committee took the precaution to prevent persons getting on the jetty from the shore. On the coming in of the first boat in the open sailing match the gun was fired, and at that moment George Potter, who had then arrived in his boat from Budleigh Salterton, clambered up on the jetty, and the cartridge entered his right side. He was removed to the Infirmary, but was not expected to survive the injuries. He has a wife and five children.*

Spread over many days, Shaldon Regatta now features gig and punt races and beach events. Strongly supported by villagers, it welcomes competitors and spectators from all over the world.

A separate event, the Water Carnival, commenced in 1922 when a flotilla of brilliantly illuminated boats passed along the Shaldon waterfront, much to the delight of spectators.

After the war, Shaldon also staged a road-based carnival that not only processed along the streets of the village, but also went out to Ringmore on its elongated circuit.

FAMOUS VISITORS

Many famous people have visited or stayed at Shaldon. Potter's Mooring, a small hotel overlooking The Green, has entertained a number of well-known guests including June Whitfield, Lenny Henry, Dawn French, and football pundit Trevor Brooking.

In the 1930s the Round House, on Marine Parade, accommodated Miss Bette Davis, the Oscar-winning Hollywood actress, whilst Sir Jimmy Savile has regularly stayed in a caravan overlooking the Teign estuary.

SHALDON AT WAR

Generally speaking, Shaldon's appeal is that it is a quiet, relaxing place. However, there have been times when it was far from peaceful. On 2 August 1943, a German war plane dropped a bomb, which landed on the bowling green and bounced over the roofs of nearby houses before exploding on the allotments. The bang was so terrific that it momentarily lifted the roof on Peartree Cottage, but, surprisingly, left the windows intact! The tail of this bomb came off with the initial impact and could be seen sticking out of the ground like a shark's fin. Most assumed that this was another, unexploded bomb, a situation that caused excitement and no little confusion until the truth was eventually discovered.

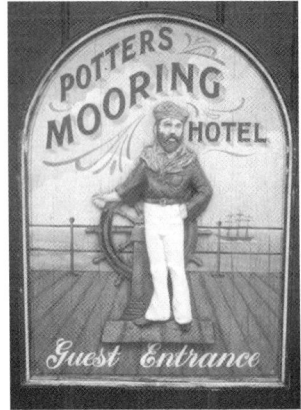

During this raid another bomb hit the beach with such force that it created a crater as big as a double decker bus. Amazingly, nobody was hurt.

An attractive brick-built clocktower sited near The Green serves as a monument to the dead of the two World Wars.

GHOSTLY GOINGS-ON!

The district has its ghosts. In Ringmore Road there is a haunted property, originally two small cottages but now amalgamated into one. An old fisherman haunts what used to be the dining room. He is only fleetingly seen out of the corner of the eye, but has been half-spied many times.

This old picture postcard opposite (top) shows the forking of two roads: Ringmore Road to the left, leading towards Shaldon, and Topcliff Road to the right, heading in the same general direction. It is said that the ghost of a spectral black dog has been seen along the latter. There are fewer trees along it now, so perhaps that's why it hasn't been seen in recent years!

GOOD NEWS, BAD NEWS

In the past shipbuilding took place at Ringmore. This was possible prior to the building of the first Shaldon Bridge (1827) because a deep water channel also existed on the southern side of the river. Some of the vessels used against the French in the Napoleonic wars began their lives here.

However, the construction of the bridge interfered with the course and nature of the river; the deep water channel began to silt and became too shallow. The shipbuilding industry died, taking with it the livelihoods of many local people – but at least people could cross the river to Teignmouth!

SLEEPY RINGMORE?

Someone once wrote that: *Sleepy Ringmore had a charm of its own – it smelled of dog-roses, honeysuckle, apples and farmyards and the orchards and fields had not been built over – it was open sweet smelling country.* However, sometimes it smelled of smoke…

Under the heading "Residents Roused By Strange Noise" this appeared in the local press on 4 January 1939: *Miss Paine and her mother, who is well over the age of 80, of Pear Tree Cottage, Ringmore, Shaldon, were awakened in the early morning by a noise they took to be made by the owls that have lived in their chimney for years. When they found their living room filling with smoke, however, they realised that it was something more than the owls. The dining room was also full of smoke.*

As it is a thatched house, Miss Paine went at once to the fire alarm at the top of Church-hill to summon the Teignmouth Brigade. Although it was 3 am, the engine arrived in a short time, and the trouble was found to be a smouldering beam across the chimney. It is thought that it had been in this state for several days.

Pear Tree Cottage is a very old house, and if once the fire had taken hold would have soon been destroyed, but fortunately Miss Paine's prompt action prevented much damage. Several neighbours offered to take Miss Paine into their houses, but she refused to leave, and was concerned chiefly with making PC Woolland, who had been called to the scene, a nice cup of tea.

ALL THE WAY TO LABRADOR

The same thirsty policeman had also attended another fire the previous year when the Labrador Bay Hotel burnt down to smouldering embers. He didn't get 'a nice cup of tea' then. The address of the former hotel always included Shaldon to qualify its whereabouts, but those looking for it in the village were wasting their time. Quite a considerable walk, over some steep cliffs, was needed to reach it on foot. Those who wished to drive there were obliged to climb out of Shaldon on the coast road towards Maidencombe. A mile or more out of the village, and tucked hundreds of feet below the coast road, access to it for large vehicles was a problem. This is how the press reported the story of its demise on April Fool's Day 1938: *Damage estimated at several thousand pounds was done in the early hours of Friday, when the Labrador Bay Hotel, which lies at the foot of the road between Shaldon and Torquay was gutted by fire. Originally a cottage that was reputed to be 300 years old and a haunt for smugglers, the only approaches to the hotel are down the cliff via 400 steps, or by sea, and this difficulty of access prevented the Teignmouth Fire Brigade from getting its appliances at work on the outbreak.*

The fire-engines had to be left in the roadway at the top of the cliff, and members of the Brigade were limited in their efforts to fight the fire with buckets and biscuit tins of water – a hopeless task in the face of the extent of the conflagration. Nevertheless they never flagged in their efforts, and tributes to their speedy arrival and work were paid to our representative by Mr A. T. Howell, the manager, who, with his wife, was residing at the hotel.

Mr Howell stated that he and his wife owed their lives to an open window. Shortly before 5 o'clock he was awakened by smoke blowing into his room, and on investigation found that the back staircase was ablaze, but they managed to get to the front staircase and escape, in the scantiest attire, to give the alarm.

Within another quarter of an hour Mr Howell thought they might have been trapped.

The roof of the building was of thatch, and it was thought that the fire may have been due to a faulty flue, although Mr Howell stated that when he retired at 11.30 overnight nothing seemed

Labrador, near Teignmouth

amiss. When the smoke had spent itself, all that remained of what had been a pretty picture, especially from the shore of Labrador Bay (a favourite spot for summer visitors), were smoking material, a charred bath, &c but practically untouched were a few pounds of butter, some cakes of soap, ice-cream glasses, and a few chairs.

It is likely that the butter had been contained in a refrigerator which exploded during the fire, and a consequence of which Chief Officer Rowe narrowly escaped injury from flying fragments.

Mr Howell further informed our representative that the hotel was fully booked up for the summer season.

In addition to the fire brigade, a number of police officers were on the scene, including Sergeant Squires and PCs Minter and Perryman (Teignmouth) and PC Woolland (Shaldon).

Headed "History of Labrador", this article was published in the local press on 16 April 1916 and provides some interesting details: *It seems that this delightful old place was built in 1630 by a certain Captain Trapp, a cod trader between the real Labrador and Teignmouth Port.*

His selection of such a site for a haven of rest after his long voyages suggests that the old sea-dog had artistic tastes in addition to those in other directions. Captain Trapp lived thirteen years to enjoy his new Labrador. After his death the house remained apparently vacant for some years, being used by the local sailors as a convenient place to land and store contraband, and some lively times were experienced for the next ten years or so.

No record exists of an owner or tenant until the advent of a Jacobean spy, named Pierre Ducress, who had lived at Labrador for several years previous to the celebrated raid on Teignmouth in 1696.

Subsequently this led to another raid on Labrador by the local populace, and the said Pierre Ducress suddenly found Labrador "unhealthy" for a boat and what possessions he could remove vanished a few days later.

It is still supposed that much loot is buried at Labrador, several old cannon and other articles of interest having been disinterred there from time to time.

Another blank space occurs until 1740, when a Cornish fisherman, named Treloar, was detected by the Preventive officers in a too enthusiatic desire to quench the thirsts of the Teignmouth folk at a more reasonable cost than the Government of the time allowed. We understand he afterwards "visited the Antipodes."

In 1758 Labrador was passing through more peaceful times under the direction of a potato farmer, but shortly after the ideal position again tempted lace merchants to depot their wares at Labrador. This comparatively peaceful trade developing a side line of brandy, etc, again roused objection with the Revenue, and some goodly fights were a rather common occurrence between 1760 and 1800.

It is not generally known that the "Bellerophon," with the Emperor Napoleon on board, very nearly went ashore near Labrador while on her way to Torbay in 1815...

In 1820 Labrador became a goat farm... Once again the old cliff path attracted the attention of smugglers, and the old place fell into decay until 1850, when an Aberystwyth gentleman purchased Labrador to convert into a private residence. This gentleman built on to the old place what is now known as "Honeymoon Cottage," and brought Labrador up to date.

Labrador subsequently became an inn, and conducted itself in a more or less respectable

Labrador Cottage

manner until a member of the London Stock Exchange purchased it in 1909, and immediately surrendered the license. A large sum of money was expended putting in fruit trees, the cable lift, etc, and Labrador to-day stands highly in the estimation of thousands of visitors.

The present proprietor has done much to enhance the reputation of Labrador, which bids fair to become "the" attraction of the South Devon Coast.

But the anonymous writer of the article did not have the benefit of a crystal ball to predict its fate of 1938.

IN CONCLUSION

Although Shaldon warmly welcomes its summer visitors, it also enjoys its quieter winter months. This is nothing new, as Mr Harper, a travel writer, made these observations in 1909: *Shaldon, however is very much of a backwater, or still pool of life, and when the visitors are gone, when the children have deserted the warm sands, and the half-dozen ferry boats are reduced to two; and when nature, with autumn past, frugally turns the lights down until next spring, Shaldon is apt to be dull. But there is always the harbour to look out upon...*

Shaldon remains a lively and colourful place in summer. With its weekly summer celebration of '1785 Day' (Wednesdays, May to September), the brainchild of the Revd Ashley Manhire, Shaldon reflects its past. The charity-raising event was commenced in 1985 when local historians felt that it mirrored the time when Shaldon began to evolve as a settlement. Guided walks provide an excellent insight the village's past and help to put '1785 Day' into some sort of perspective.

A colourful crafts market is held at The Green with many excellent stalls on view. Holidaymakers like to indulge in some fun by posing in the stocks. It provides them with a fond memory of their time in Shaldon, and also raises money for good causes.

Shaldon appeals to sociable sailors and thirsty fishermen. It's hard concisely to sum up exactly what Shaldon is all about, but a possible definition put forward by an astute local person goes some of the way towards defining the spirit or character of the place: he said that it was "A quaint little drinking village with a fishing problem." Cheers!